Fearfully and Wonderfully Me
Become the Woman You are Destined to Be
WORKBOOK

RIA STORY

Copyright © 2020 Ria Story
All rights reserved.

ISBN-13: 9798648551954

WHAT OTHERS ARE SAYING ABOUT RIA AND HER BOOKS:

"I want to start by saying thank you...You made me want to try at life because you made me realize that you can make it anywhere you want, no matter where or what you are from. THANK YOU SO MUCH!" JONATHAN, HIGH SCHOOL STUDENT

"Ria's book (Beyond Bound and Broken) is full of hope and inspiration, and she shows us that despite experiencing horrific trauma as a young adult, that if we choose to, we can get past anything with the attitude that we bring to our life...Her book is full of wonderful quotes and wisdom."
MADELEINE BLACK, AUTHOR OF UNBROKEN

"I am using your material to empower myself and my female clients. Thanks for sharing your story and a wonderful journey of growth."
SUE QUIGLEY, LICENSED CLINICAL THERAPIST

"Very few 'victims' would be willing to share such a personal story. However, nothing about Ria is average. She chose to rise above her painful past and now positions it in a way to offer hope and healing to others who've been through unspeakable abuse. Ria's faith and marriage keep her grounded as she reveals the solid foundation which helps her stand as an overcomer. Read this story and find yourself and your own story strengthened."
KARY OBERBRUNNER, AUTHOR AND FOUNDER OF AUTHOR ACADEMY ELITE, ON RIA'S STORY FROM ASHES TO BEAUTY

"Thank you, Ria, for bringing our conference to a close. You were definitely an inspiration to all of us! Awesome Job!"
MELINDA, PRESIDENT AGS

"Beyond Bound and Broken is a deeply inspirational book; one that will stay with you for years to come. The lessons are deep, yet practical, and her advice leads to clear solutions. This is a profoundly hopeful book. We all face pain, difficulty, and doubt but with resilience, we can lead vital, flourishing lives. Ria's story although sometimes painfully difficult to read because of the trials she endured is a story of great courage and compassion both for herself as victim and for those who betrayed her. Forgiveness is a strong theme as is courage. I would highly recommend this book to anyone who is struggling to move forward after experiencing a great trial." AMAZON CUSTOMER

"…it was awesome! Ria has a real gift. I came away with so many helpful tools! Thank you, Ria."
STEFANIE, CONFERENCE ATTENDEE

"May God continue to bless your efforts. Your triumph is a great joy, and a gift to all that would hear or read it."
LOUIS O., HUMAN RIGHTS ADVOCATE

"What an inspiration you are to all of us especially the women audience. Your book is a clear example & step by step guide on how to become an effective leader. It is so easy to read and simple yet meaningful which is the beauty of this book."
K. POONWALA, CUSTOMER SUCCESS MANAGER, ON LEADERSHIP GEMS FOR WOMEN

"I was truly inspired by your presentation and the life lessons taught."
JENNIFER, CONFERENCE ATTENDEE

See more testimonials at:
riastory.com/testimonials

DEDICATION

To women all over the world:

We cannot change everything, but we always have the power to change ourselves.

May you have peace about the things you cannot change, the courage to change yourself, and the wisdom to understand changing yourself changes the world.

And, may you love yourself enough to do so.

CONTENTS

	Introduction	i
1	Fearfully and Wonderfully Me	1
2	You are *Destined* to be *More*	5
3	Moving Beyond the Victim Mindset	9
4	No Excuse for Excuses	13
5	Leadership and Influence	17
6	Leadership vs Management	21
7	Embrace the Leader Within	25
8	The Female Advantage	29
9	Self-Belief: I am responsible.	33
10	Self-Belief: I can change _____ .	37
11	Self-Belief: I can grow beyond trauma.	41
12	Self-Worth: I am a miracle.	45
13	Self-Worth: I create my identity.	49
14	Self-Worth: I am "Me" first.	53
15	Self-Love: I love myself.	57

16	Self-Love: I love my potential.	61
17	Self-Love: I am becoming better.	65
18	Self-Respect: I choose my values.	69
19	Self-Respect: I focus on myself.	73
20	Self-Respect: I define my boundaries.	77
21	Self-Care: I am disciplined.	81
22	Self-Care: I create my habits.	85
23	Self-Care: I take small steps every day.	89
24	Self-Development: I develop my leadership daily.	93
25	Self-Development: I increase my influence daily.	97
26	Self-Development: I will maximize my results daily.	101
27	Self-Realization: I will make a difference.	105
28	Self-Realization: I will achieve success.	109
29	Self-Realization: I am living my legacy.	113
30	Transformation Happens Daily, Not in a Day	117

INTRODUCTION

As I began writing *Fearfully and Wonderfully Me: Become the Woman You are Destined to Be*, the biggest challenge I faced was how to help you actually apply the concepts to your own life and situation. The principles in the book are life-changing (I'm living proof) **when they are applied.** They didn't do me any good until I started applying them to my life, and they won't do you any good until you start applying them to yours.

As much as I want to, I can't do it for you. *Fearfully and Wonderfully Me: Become the Woman You are Destined to Be* (FWM) isn't a book about what you should *do* differently in order to reach your goals, achieve your dreams, and *become* the woman and leader you are destined to *be*. It's about *how to BE* different in order to accomplish those things. Or, I should say, *how to become*. But, you must do the work. And, it will be work.

Becoming the best version of you, whatever that looks like, will require personal transformation. You must transform from who you are now into who you have the potential to *become*.

And, that starts with mindset.

If all you do is read the book, nothing will change. You must apply the principles to benefit from them. To help with this, I created a few accompanying worksheets and included them in the back of FWM. And, I provided extra blank copies of these worksheets on my website in the event you wanted to use them again in the future. (Or, if you just have a hang-up about writing in an actual book.)

I wanted FWM to be a stand-alone resource, because I know many people only need a spark to get started. But, I also realized some people want, and need, a more comprehensive resource. Perhaps you want more coaching and support as you travel your personal transformation journey. Perhaps you want to accelerate your pace. And, you realize a deeper dive will help you go faster.

If so, I created this accompanying workbook for you.

You will need a few things on our journey.

You will need a copy of FWM. Order that now, if you don't already have it. You will be missing some key information if you try to only go through this workbook alone.

You will need to read the corresponding chapter in FWM before you complete the worksheet. For example, before you complete the worksheet in chapter 1 of this workbook, read chapter 1 of FWM. Then, you will have the right perspective for the reflection questions as you complete the worksheets.

And, you will need belief in yourself and your potential.

When you intentionally change your thoughts, your thoughts will automatically change your life.

Now, let's take a journey together.

Chapter One

FEARFULLY AND WONDERFULLY ME

"Who you are gives birth to who you may become."

~ Ria Story

We often create self-limiting beliefs based on insecurities. These insecurities could be physical, emotional, social, or even spiritual. But, in truth, we are "Fearfully and Wonderfully" created in the image of God.

1) What insecurities do I have about myself?

2) What "body" issues do I have?

3) When have these beliefs held me back?

4) How has this affected my relationships?

5) What will be possible if I don't allow these limiting beliefs to hold me back any longer? What will be better?

6) What is <u>one</u> thing I will do differently after reading chapter one and reflecting on the workbook questions from this chapter?

Chapter Two

YOU ARE DESTINED TO BE MORE

"You don't have to be sick to get better."

~ Michael Josephson

There is nothing wrong with you. But, we always have potential to improve ourselves and therefore our circumstances. Becoming "better" simply means *becoming* the woman and leader you are destined to *be*. It's tapping into your potential to do more, have more, and *be* more. Every woman's definition of "better" is unique to her.

1) What does my definition of "better" look like?

2) How do I want to be "better" physically? How could my health be better?

3) How do I want to be "better" mentally or emotionally?

4) How will my relationships be better?

5) How would I like to be "better" spiritually?

6) How will I benefit by becoming better?

7) What is one thing I can do every day to become better?

Chapter Three

MOVING BEYOND THE VICTIM MINDSET

"No one else has as much influence in your life as you do."
~ Ria Story

What happens to us doesn't matter as much as what we decide to do about what happens to us. **You don't have to make bad choices** that hold you back from your goals, your dreams, and your life because of what happened to you, or what someone said to you, or what you went through. To reach your potential, you must move beyond the victim mindset.

1) What trauma have I experienced? When did I experience pain?

2) Why or how does this trauma keep me from choosing joy?

3) How has this affected me <u>negatively</u>?

4) How has this affected me <u>positively</u>?

5) What are some methods I have used to heal? How have they helped?

6) What else will help me heal?

Chapter Four

NO EXCUSE FOR EXCUSES

"An excuse is our reality only because we make it so."
~ Ria Story

Personal responsibility is the key to overcoming our excuses. We must take ownership of our choices in order to improve our results, circumstances, and our lives. Excuses don't serve your dreams.

1) What excuses have I created about why I can't do what I want to do, have what I want to have, or be what I want to be? (include statements like, "I can't do _____because of _____.")

2) How are my excuses holding me back?

3) What coping methods or behaviors have I used when I make excuses?

4) What will I try instead?

5) How do my excuses affect other people?

6) How do my emotions affect others? When do my fears affect others? My anger? My shame?

Chapter Five

LEADERSHIP AND INFLUENCE

"Influencing others begins with us having the ability to lead and influence ourselves first."

~ Ria Story

Life gets better when we have more influence. With more influence comes more options and better opportunities. Life will always be easier when we have more options and better opportunities.

1) How are my physical choices affecting my influence? (positively or negatively)

2) How are my mental/emotional choices affecting my influence? (positively or negatively)

3) How are my spiritual choices affecting my influence? (positively or negatively)

4) How are my relationship choices affecting my influence? (positively or negatively)

5) Who do I want to have more influence with?

6) How will my influence increase if I lead myself better?

Chapter Six

LEADERSHIP VS MANAGEMENT

"Management relates to managing things, projects, and processes. Leadership relates to leading and influencing people."

~ Ria Story

Things, projects, and processes don't have feelings, thoughts, opinions or emotions. People do. When we fail to account for and respect those feelings, thoughts, and emotions, we stop leading, start managing, and begin to lose influence.

1) Do I have a natural tendency toward being focused on tasks or people?

2) Do I value influencing people?

3) How do I lead my children? My coworkers or team members? My spouse? My friends?

4) Do I try to influence them, or do I try to manage them by simply telling them what to do?

5) Who has influenced and inspired me as a positive role model in my life?

6) Who do I know who is good at influencing people? What makes them effective?

Chapter Seven

EMBRACE THE LEADER WITHIN

"We can be a different type of leader to different people based on our relationship with them."

~ Ria Story

There are four types of leaders and each of us has the potential to grow through each phase during our leadership journey.

1) Who is on my team? When I need help, who can I trust?

2) Where do I show up as a Conductor? Who would say I'm a Conductor?

3) Where do I show up as a Connector? Who would say I'm a Connector?

4) Where do I show up as a Compounder? Who would say I'm a Compounder?

5) Where do I show up as a Catalyst? Who would say I'm a Catalyst?

6) Who has been a Catalyst in my life? What changes did I make because of them?

Chapter Eight

THE FEMALE ADVANTAGE

"Relationship determines influence because both influence and relationships are built on trust.

~ Ria Story

The key to influencing others is developing our character, focusing on our own personal growth, and expanding our influence based more on *who we are* than *what we do*.

1) Who do I have a healthy relationship with?

2) What relationships in my life do I need to focus on improving?

3) How will I increase my influence in my relationships?

4) What do I need to do differently to build trust?

5) What do I like about who I am as a person?

6) What would I like to change about who I am as a person?

Chapter Nine

SELF-BELIEF: I AM RESPONSIBLE

"Who you will be tomorrow is based on the choices you make today."
~ Ria Story

The moment we accept responsibility for our choices is the moment we discover the freedom to change our circumstances.

1) What do I want to change in my life?

2) What am I unhappy about?

3) What choices have I made in the past that could possibly have created this situation or contributed to this situation?

4) What can I do to influence this situation? What's stopping me from doing it?

5) What would I do differently if I could do things over?

6) What do I want to do now to move forward? What's stopping me?

Chapter Ten

SELF-BELIEF: I CAN CHANGE _____

"You can change almost anything if you are willing to put in the work and pay the price."

~ Ria Story

If you truly cannot change something, move on. You can't change it. Quit worrying about it. Quit stressing over it. Quit focusing on it. But, most things can be changed or influenced by what we do, although it may not change immediately.

1) What is one thing I want to achieve?

2) What are all the actions I can take that would help me achieve it?

3) Which of these actions am I 100% committed to doing?

4) Which of these actions will I do every day? List 3-5 things you will do every day to move forward.

5) What would or could stop me from doing these things every day? What are the potential roadblocks I might face?

6) How can I make sure that doesn't happen? How can I navigate around the roadblocks?

Chapter Eleven

SELF-BELIEF: I CAN GROW BEYOND TRAUMA

"Trauma creates an opportunity to grow."

~ Ria Story

Reflection in search of lessons is what allows you to begin turning trauma into growth.

1) In what ways have I grown since the trauma I experienced?

2) What did I learn about myself?

3) What did I learn about others?

4) In what way can I turn this adversity into my advantage?

5) What are the positives that came from this situation?

6) What would I like to say about my traumatic experience?

Chapter Twelve

SELF-WORTH: I AM A MIRACLE

"Your self-worth should be based on the recognition that you have inherent value as a special human being created purposefully by God."
~ Ria Story

We create the "frame" in which we see ourselves. And, since we are the framer, we can change the frame. In other words, we can change our perspective of ourselves to a positive one. And, when we choose to view ourselves as precious, valuable, and worthy, we choose to take better care of ourselves. Imagine a picture frame on the wall, and inside it is a picture of you. Keep that in mind as you answer these questions.

1) What does my picture "frame" look like? Is constructed with happy thoughts? Sad thoughts? Angry thoughts? Other thoughts?

2) When did I create this "frame" of myself?

3) Is this the frame I want to keep?

4) What will happen if I change the "frame" of myself to a more positive one?

5) What negative things do I tell myself?

6) Write down the opposite of those negative things as positive affirmations. (Download free affirmations at: RiaStory.com/affirmations)

Chapter Thirteen

SELF-WORTH: I CREATE MY IDENTITY

"No one can create your identity except you."

~ Ria Story

Who you want to *be* is something you *can* determine. We are not determined by others, only influenced by them. You must be intentional about creating your own identity, instead of allowing it to be shaped by other influences.

1) What coping mechanisms have I used/am I using to numb pain, fear, or trauma?

2) How has this influenced my identity?

3) What should I do differently instead?

4) What do I need in order to heal?

5) When people describe who I am as a person, I want them to say:

6) What principles are important to me in creating my identity?

Chapter Fourteen

SELF-WORTH: I AM "ME" FIRST

"You can't be everything to everyone, and you can't be the best version of you unless you remember to be you first."

~ Ria Story

You won't have lasting confidence if you try to form your identity around being attractive, wealthy, or the best at your job because those things may not last. Then, your identity will crumble when they fade away. Form your identity around principles, and you will be much better equipped to make the right choices at the right time for the right reasons.

1) What "hats" do I wear? List 2-7 but no more than that.

2) What boundaries will I set to make sure these "hats" don't become my core identity?

3) What do I want to form my core identify on? (Let your most important values such as family, health etc. guide you to identify the related principles.)

4) What do I want my life to look like in 5 years?

5) Because I love myself, I will take care of myself. For me, self-care looks like:

6) When I'm tired, feeling drained, anxious, or depleted, these things will help me rest and regenerate:

Chapter Fifteen

SELF-LOVE: I LOVE MYSELF

"What happens to us in life is not as important as who we become because of it."

~ Ria Story

Loving yourself and your story takes courage. To really love yourself is to acknowledge your flaws, mistakes, imperfections, past hurts, traumatic experiences and the insecurities they caused. When you own your story, it can't own you. How the next chapter is written is up to you.

1) What part of my past am I still holding on to that I need to let go of?

2) What do I need to forgive myself for?

3) What do I need to forgive others for?

4) How will things be better when I let go of past bitterness, resentment, trauma, pain, or adversity?

5) What character flaws do I want to overcome? (not keeping commitments, lack of integrity, etc.)

6) How did my past help positively shape who I am today?

7) What helps me feel safe? Feel loved?

Chapter Sixteen

SELF-LOVE:
I LOVE MY POTENTIAL

"Everything we've created in the world started first as a vision inside someone's head."

~ Ria Story

If we don't have hope that the future will be better, we won't have a reason to do things differently. You must *believe* in yourself, your potential, and your power to convert your vision into your reality.

1) What brings me joy?

2) What do I do better than anyone else I know?

3) What have I been dreaming about doing? What do I feel called to do?

4) What am I so passionate about doing that I will do it for free?

5) Is this something that there is a need for? Is this a potential business I could start? Is it a career or just a hobby?

6) What advice should I give myself about this?

Chapter Seventeen

SELF-LOVE: I AM BECOMING BETTER

"Every moment brings possibility and the potential to take us closer to or farther away from our destination."

~ Ria Story

Becoming better is about becoming better every day in some way. It's about leveraging the power of making better choices in the moment to create great minutes, great hours, great days, great years, and a great life.

1) What have I sacrificed in the past to get to where I am today?

2) What am I holding on to right now that is holding me back?

3) What am I willing to sacrifice in order to become closer to MY version of "better?"

4) What will the long term gains be when I make the short term sacrifice?

5) How can I make one better choice today? (make sure to focus on something small and easily achievable, but also be specific)

6) What will I do when I make a mistake? How will I ensure it doesn't get me off track permanently?

Chapter Eighteen

SELF-RESPECT: I CHOOSE MY VALUES

"If you won't invest in yourself, why should anyone else? Make it happen!"

~ Ria Story

We make our choices, then our choices make us. We can choose our thoughts, mindset, attitude, values, and actions, but the consequences that flow from those choices will be automatic, positive or negative.

1) My top five values are:

2) If I choose only two, they will be:

3) Do I value my health? What do my choices reveal?

4) Do I value family time? What does my calendar reveal?

5) Do I value saving money for hard times? What does my bank account reveal?

6) Do I value improving my circumstances and increasing my influence with others? What do my reading and personal growth habits reveal?

Chapter Nineteen

SELF-RESPECT: I FOCUS ON MYSELF

"Nothing great is ever accomplished with little effort."
~ Ria Story

You cannot change or transform anyone else. You cannot control anyone else. You cannot "improve" someone else. All you can do is focus on improving yourself and increasing your influence. Transformation begins with you. It's between you and you.

1) Which relationships do I find most frustrating due to the behavior of the other person?

2) What will I do to focus on myself in this situation instead of trying to "fix" the other person?

3) Is this a healthy relationship for me? How can I improve it?

4) Who looks up to me? Who am I a role model for?

5) How will I be a better role model?

6) How will I become a better listener?

Chapter Twenty

SELF-RESPECT: I DEFINE MY BOUNDARIES

"Boundaries are the acceptable limits within which choices are made."
~ Ria Story

Personal boundaries are limits we determine, set, and create for ourselves. Relational boundaries are limits we determine, set, and create with others.

1) What areas of my life do I excel in setting and keeping my personal boundaries?

2) What areas of my life do I struggle with personal boundaries? (such as eating, exercise, too much T.V., social media, etc.)

3) What will help me be more successful in these areas? (accountability, coaching, etc.)

4) What areas of my life do I excel in setting boundaries in relationships?

5) Which areas do I struggle to set or keep boundaries in relationships?

6) What are some things I will do to help me be more effective in setting or keeping relational boundaries?

Chapter Twenty-One

SELF-CARE: I AM DISCIPLINED

"Self-discipline is your foundation for future success."
~ Ria Story

Self-discipline is making choices proactively with your head instead of reactively with your heart or emotions or automatically through your habits.

1) Which areas of life do I do well with self-discipline? (physically such as healthy habits, emotionally such as growth habits, socially such as keeping commitments to others, etc.)

2) Which areas of my life do I struggle with the most relative to self-discipline?

3) Why is this area challenging for me?

4) What usually happens to derail my self-discipline? (is there a pattern or trigger?)

5) How will I break down my commitments into more achievable (smaller) steps to ensure I am 100% committed?

6) How will my life be better when I do?

Chapter Twenty-Two

SELF-CARE: I CREATE MY HABITS

"Habits are created by the choices we repeatedly make."
~ Ria Story

Habits can help us or hurt us. Make a list on this page of your habits. Habits you consider positive and habits you consider negative.

1) Which of these habits are helping me become the woman I want to be?

2) Which of these habits ARE NOT helping me become the woman I want to be? (Remember, there is no judgement here. Just awareness and reflection.)

3) Which habit will I change or improve?

4) What is the trigger for this habit? (what happens to cue my behavior?)

5) What action or behavior will I replace this habit with? What will help me? (remember to start small!)

Chapter Twenty-Three

SELF-CARE: I TAKE SMALL STEPS EVERY DAY

"When you choose to do better, you will BE better."
~ Ria Story

Creating good habits is about learning to control yourself. Master the small things first, and the big things won't seem so big.

1) What do I want the first few minutes of my day to be like?

2) What's my morning routine to ensure my day starts well?

3) How will I simplify my life in one little way today?

4) What are three things I would like to do more of in the future?

5) What advice should I give myself about my daily choices and habits?

6) Who can help me be more intentional about my choices and habits? Who can help me with accountability?

Chapter Twenty-Four

SELF-DEVELOPMENT: I DEVELOP MY LEADERSHIP DAILY

"We must choose the right values and have the integrity to live true to them."

~ Ria Story

Character must be developed daily. And, it *can't* be developed in a single day. The great thing is we don't have to get it right all the time. We simply must ask ourselves, "How can I get better today?"

1) How will my influence increase overall if I develop my character a little bit every day?

2) What three things will I do **every day** to develop my character? (read a paragraph in a leadership book, listen to a podcast, etc.)

3) Who in my life do I want to be intentional about building more influence with? (Choose one to three relationships.)

4) How will I intentionally add value to these relationships?

5) Who would I most like to increase my influence with in this season of my life? (choose one: children, spouse, boss, etc.)

6) What one thing will I STOP doing because it decreases my influence with this person?

Chapter Twenty-Five

SELF-DEVELOPMENT: I INCREASE MY INFLUENCE DAILY

"Become the best at what you're meant to do because that's where you will make the greatest impact in the world."

~ Ria Story

When it comes to *character,* we should absolutely work on our weaknesses because those weaknesses will hold us back in life. But, when it comes to *competency,* we should hone our strengths because those skills will help us shine like a diamond.

1) What are my gifts? What do I naturally do very well? Where and when do I excel?

2) What brings me joy when I do it? What am I passionate about?

3) What will people pay me to do that I am passionate about doing?

4) What competencies would help me increase my influence? (such as certification in a technical skill, college degree, or becoming a subject matter expert in a field, etc.)

5) Who can mentor me in this area? (Mentorship could be in person or by reading books on experts in the subject.)

6) What do I feel called to do?

Chapter Twenty-Six

SELF-DEVELOPMENT: I WILL MAXIMIZE MY RESULTS DAILY

"The way you act affirms your belief in who you are becoming."
~ Ria Story

Every choice, action, deed, and word (spoken to yourself or someone else) is like one tiny brick in a massive cathedral. And, if you imagine the best version of yourself as a beautiful cathedral, you're building it one brick at a time with every choice you make, every action you take, every deed you do, and every word you speak.

1) What will I change in my environment to help me make better choices?

2) Who will I spend LESS time with to become the best version of myself?

3) Who will I spend MORE time with to become the best version of myself?

4) How would the person I want to become start their day? End their day?

5) What else would that person do throughout their day?

6) What will help me get back on track when I make a poor choice?

Chapter Twenty-Seven

SELF-REALIZATION: I WILL MAKE A DIFFERENCE

"Your purpose is the one-sentence summary of how you change the world."

~ Ria Story

When we make a difference in someone's life, we find enrichment for our own. The key is to develop yourself in an effort to become more valuable by adding value to others. When you can and do make a difference, you *become* a difference-maker.

1) How would I describe my life story so far?

2) Is it falling short of what I want it to be?

3) When I look back at my story, do I see how I impacted the lives of those around me in a positive way?

4) In what ways can I add value to others? (make sure to stay in your strength zone)

5) What's one thing stopping me from doing so?

6) How will I overcome it?

Chapter Twenty-Eight

SELF-REALIZATION: I WILL ACHIEVE SUCCESS

"Ask for responsibility and steward the opportunity well. How we perform the small tasks indicates how we will perform the large tasks."

~ Ria Story

To become successful and increase your influence, take on the little jobs and do them well. Ask for more responsibility, or better yet, just do what needs to be done. Volunteer, take ownership, and gain experience because that will make you more *valuable*.

1) What "small" tasks do I find myself complaining about?

2) What will happen if I stop complaining and start performing them with a great attitude?

3) Where and when will I ask for more responsibilities and more opportunities in order to gain experience?

4) What might I learn from these experiences as I become more valuable?

5) What am I grateful for?

6) What will I do to make sure I'm practicing gratitude every day?

Chapter Twenty-Nine

SELF-REALIZATION: I AM LIVING MY LEGACY

"Becoming the best version of yourself is becoming who you were created to be and fulfilling what you were created to do."
~ Ria Story

Your legacy will remind others of who you were and what you did to help others.

1) My definition of "success" is:

2) My definition of "significance," or my legacy, is:

3) What am I willing to sacrifice or give up in order to achieve significance in the life of someone else? Time? Money? Something else?

4) What am I not willing to sacrifice?

5) Who can I help? Who should I help?

6) What will happen when I help them? To them? To me?

Chapter Thirty

TRANSFORMATION HAPPENS DAILY, NOT IN A DAY

"Our lives are our stories, and we write a chapter every day by the actions we take and the choices we make."

~ Ria Story

As a human being, you have the freedom to make choices. As time passes, the right choices will create more freedom and personal transformation. It's an uphill journey to the top of your mountain, and you are the only one who can climb it.

1) What scares me about becoming the woman I am destined to be?

2) What will I do to ensure that doesn't stop me from becoming the best version of myself?

3) What's holding me back that I am ready to let go of?

4) When I feel tempted to quit in the moment, I will do this instead:

5) What affirmations will help me?

6) Who believes in me as much, or more, than I believe in myself?

Resources for Personal Growth and Leadership Development

Access free preview chapters from Ria's other books at: RiaStory.com/Download

Find information on Ria's podcast at: RiaStory.com/Podcast

Watch Ria's TEDx talk: RiaStory.com/TEDx

Sign up for Ria's monthly newsletter: RiaStory.com

Connect with Ria on Social:

Facebook: https://www.facebook.com/ria.story
Twitter: https://twitter.com/Ria_Story
LinkedIn: https://linkedin.com/in/riastory
Instagram: https://www.instagram.com/ria.story

**Or email Ria at:
Ria@RiaStory.com**

Excerpt from *Ria's Story From Ashes To Beauty,* by Ria Story

I was 12 when Dad started having some conversations with me about the *"facts of life."* He would tell me how infidelity in marriage was wrong and so was divorce. But, *"his needs"* weren't being met because my mother wasn't able to meet them. I was told they didn't have a physical relationship for many years, but I don't know if that is true. I know she was sleeping on the couch in the living room most nights, she said because of her back. I suspect I will never know the truth. I want to believe she had no idea what was going on, but it's possible she knew and didn't want to face reality, so she shut it out. Either version is hard for me to accept, but there are many things in life we don't want to accept.

    I remember times when Mom was gone, out running errands or something, and my Dad would tell her to take my brother with her. At first, all our talks were about how I needed to be *"pure"* and stay away from boys until my Dad was able to find the *"Right one that God would send."* Then, it changed to being all about how a woman was designed by God to meet a man's needs and that was all I was created for. I remember feeling ashamed talking about things like that, but I didn't know what to do. It was the summer when I was 12 that he first started saying how a father-daughter relationship was supposed to be close in every way, physically as well as emotionally. I remember being told I was supposed to give my heart to him *"for safekeeping,"* but I was confused as to why that also meant in a physical way.

One day my Mom and brother were gone, and Dad and I were sitting in the living room *"talking."* Somehow, things turned into how wonderful it was that I was the perfect daughter and was so close to my Dad. We went upstairs, and he kept telling me how God intended for daughters to belong to daddies. And, if I would trust him, he would make sure I lived up to what God wanted. He told me how I was supposed to fill in since my Mother wasn't able to be a wife anymore. He told me I was living up to God's purpose for my life by helping him not have to commit adultery. He told me it wasn't a sin if I helped him like that. He took off my clothes and told me the whole time I was the perfect daughter.

What started out as just taking off my clothes progressed. Within a few months, it wasn't just taking off my shirt and jeans but taking off everything.

Deep in the back of a forgotten drawer, my Mom had hidden a bunch of lingerie she used to wear when she was young, and they were newly married. Dad brought it out one day while we were alone in the house together. He picked out one of the outfits and told me to go in the bathroom. Then, he wanted me to put it on and come out to model it for him. I cried afterward, ashamed of being looked at like that. I was sad for my Mom too - her personal things should not have been shared with anyone, much less her daughter.

Then, the touching started.

ORDER *RIA'S STORY FROM ASHES TO BEAUTY* ONLINE AT: AMAZON.COM OR RIASTORY.COM

Excerpt from *Straight Talk: The Power of Effective Communication,* by Ria Story

I was nearly 20 years old before I realized I liked people. I never considered myself to be an "introvert" although most people would have. I simply didn't talk to people. Ask me a question, and you would get a monosyllabic response that discouraged any further dialogue. It's not that I didn't want to talk or communicate with people – I simply didn't know how.

I grew up very isolated, living on a farm in the middle of the woods. I was homeschooled. We didn't attend church regularly, and my social contact growing up was mainly limited to field trips with other homeschoolers. In the early 1980's in Alabama, opportunities for homeschooled children to participate in extra-curricular activities were limited, and my parents didn't pursue most of them.

I was also sexually abused by my father from age 12 – 19. Growing up with feelings of shame, guilt, hurt, and unworthiness only compounded my natural tendency to be withdrawn, even after I left home at 19. I share more about my story in some of my other books, *Ria's Story From Ashes To Beauty* and *Beyond Bound and Broken: A Journey of Healing and Resilience*.

Leaving home without a job, a car, or even a high school diploma, I got a crash course on the need for communication in "normal" society.

At 19, I had a great education, ability to think critically, reasoning skills, proactive attitude, and willingness to work hard. What I didn't have was the critical ability to connect with other people and communicate *effectively*.

Since I didn't have a GED or a high school diploma,

finding a way to make a living wasn't going to be easy, but I was determined to start making money and earning my way.

My first job was working as a server at a pizza restaurant. I worked the lunch shift, Monday through Friday every day, from 11:00 – 2:00. Most customers would have the all-you-can-eat pizza and salad buffet because it was fast and didn't cost too much.

I was the only lunch server for all 36 tables in the restaurant. My job was to set up the buffet, keep the salad bar stocked and clean, make the tea, fill the ice bin, stock the soda machine, answer the phone, take delivery orders, greet the customers when they entered, take and fill their drink orders, keep dirty plates bussed, refill their drinks, check them out at the cash register, clean the tables, chairs, and floor after the customer left, wash all the dishes, put them away, and restock everything before I left. All for $2.13 per hour, plus any tips I made.

The lunch buffet was $5.99, and a drink was $1.35. Most customer bills came to less than $8.00 for lunch. The average tip is 10% for a buffet, so the best tip I could expect would be about $1.00 – and that's if I hustled really hard to keep their soda refilled and the dirty plates bussed. If I was too busy and the customer ran out of tea, I may not have gotten a tip at all.

I learned quickly that being an "introverted" waitress wasn't going to work. If I didn't smile at the customers, they thought I was unfriendly. If I didn't greet them enthusiastically, they didn't feel welcome or appreciated. If I didn't remember the names of the regular customers and what they liked to drink, they often wouldn't even leave me the change from their dollar.

I learned a lot of things during my years of waiting tables, off and on earlier in my career. You see the best and the worst of people when you wait tables. But, the most important lesson I learned was to take initiative and connect with my customers. **Communicating information wasn't enough. I had to connect with them.** I could tell them where to get a plate and take their drink order, but how I did it made all the difference in whether they left me anything at all, or sometimes, several dollars.

What I want to share with you in this book are some of the lessons I've learned about connecting with people and communicating effectively. There aren't any shortcuts to success, but I hope I can help you avoid the detours and map out a faster route.

Effective communication skills are critical to our success in life.

On the professional side, the ability to communicate and relate to customers, co-workers, employees, or your boss can determine your career potential and define your success.

On the personal side, communication with your spouse, children, parents, and friends will determine your satisfaction in life (at least some of it) and define your relationships.

Regardless of your preferred personality style, or whether you consider yourself an introvert or extrovert, dealing with other people is a fact of life. Almost any situation you can think of requires you to come in contact and interact with other people sooner or later.

Your eye color cannot be changed. Your genetic ability to run a four-minute mile cannot be changed. Your ability to communicate CAN be changed. **Communication is a skill anyone can learn, and everyone can learn to do it better.**

ABOUT THE AUTHOR

Like many, Ria faced adversity in life. Ria was sexually abused by her father from age 12 - 19, forced to play the role of his wife, and even shared with other men. Desperate to escape, she left home at 19 without a job, a car, or even a high school diploma. Ria learned to be resilient, not only surviving, but thriving. She worked her way through college, earning her MBA with a cumulative 4.0 GPA, and had a successful career in the corporate world of administrative healthcare.

Ria's background includes more than 10 years in administrative healthcare including working as the Director of Compliance for a large healthcare organization. Ria's responsibilities included oversight of thousands of organizational policies, organizational compliance with all State and Federal regulations, and responsibility for several million dollars in Medicare appeals.

Today, Ria is a motivational leadership speaker, TEDx Speaker, and author of 20 books and journals, including Leadership Gems for Women. Ria is a certified leadership speaker and trainer and was selected three times to speak on stage at International John Maxwell Certification Events. Motivational speaker Les Brown also invited Ria to share the stage with him in Los Angeles, CA.

Ria has a passion for health and wellness and is a certified group fitness instructor. She has completed several marathons and half-marathons and won both the Alabama and Georgia Women's State Mountain Biking Championships in 2011 and 2012.

Ria shares powerful leadership principles and tools of transformation from her journey to equip and empower women, helping them maximize their potential in life and leadership.

ABOUT MACK STORY

Mack's story is an amazing journey of personal and professional growth. He married Ria in 2001. He has one son, Eric, born in 1991.

After graduating high school in 1987, Mack joined the USMC Reserves as an 0311 infantryman. Soon after in 1988, he began his 20 plus year manufacturing career on the front lines of a large production machine shop. Graduating with highest honors, he earned an Executive Bachelor of Business Administration degree from Faulkner University in 2002. He eventually grew himself into upper management and found his niche in lean manufacturing and along with it, developed his passion for leadership. In 2008, he launched his own Lean Manufacturing and Leadership Development business.

From 2005-2012, Mack led leaders and their cross-functional teams through more than 11,000 hours of process improvement, organizational change, and cultural transformation. In 2013, Mack and Ria served with John C. Maxwell as part of Cultural Transformation in Guatemala where over 20,000 leaders were trained. They also shared the stage with internationally recognized motivational speaker Les Brown in 2014. In 2018, they were invited to speak at Yale University's School of Management.

Mack has also published 13 books on personal growth and leadership development including his five very popular *Blue-Collar Leadership® Series* books.

Mack and Ria inspire people everywhere through their example of achievement, growth, and personal development.

Clients: ATD (Association for Talent Development), Auburn University, Chevron, Chick-fil-A, Kimberly Clark, Koch Industries, Southern Company, and the U.S. Military.

Resources for Recovery

If you have experienced sexual assault or abuse or know of a loved one who has, there are resources available to help. You are not alone!

National Sexual Assault Hotline:
800-656-HOPE (4673)

Visit: www.centers.rainn.org to search for a local crisis center in your area.

Rape, Abuse, & Incest National Network has information and resources available on their website:
www.rainn.org

Department of Defense/Military Support:
www.safehelpline.org or 877-995-5247

National Sexual Violence Resource Center:
www.nsvrc.org

Read more books by Ria

In *Beyond Bound and Broken*, Ria shares how she overcame the shame, fear, and doubt she developed after enduring years of extreme sexual abuse by her father. Forced to play the role of a wife and even shared with other men due to her father's perversions, Ria left home at 19 without a job, a car, or even a high-school diploma. This book also contains lessons on resilience and overcoming adversity that you can apply to your own life.

In *Ria's Story From Ashes To Beauty*, Ria tells her personal story of growing up as a victim of extreme sexual abuse from age 12 – 19, leaving home to escape, and her decision to tell her story.

Read more books by Ria

The Ladder of Influence provides a powerful, yet simple, framework to help you realize the practical steps you can take to increase your influence with the people around you: family, friends, co-workers, your boss, etc.

We all have some influence, yet we all want more influence. Simple. But why, how, where, who, and when we influence others as well as how we in turn are influenced by others is incredibly complex because people are incredibly complex.

When we have more influence, we have more options, opportunities, and more choices. Life will always be better with more options, more opportunities, and more choices.

Order books online at Amazon or RiaStory.com

It's not what happens to you in life. It's who you become because of it. We all experience pain, grief, and loss in life. Resilience is the difference between *"I didn't die,"* and *"I learned to live again."* In this captivating book on resilience, Ria walks you through her own horrific story of more than seven years of sexual abuse by her father. She then shares how she learned not only to survive, but also to thrive in spite of her past. Learn how to overcome challenges, obstacles, and adversity in your own life by building a bridge out of the past and into the future.

(Watch 7 minutes of her story at RiaStory.com/TEDx)

Motivational Planning Journals
Choose a theme for the season of your life!
Now available at Amazon.com or RiaStory.com

Start each day with a purposeful mindset, and you will achieve your priorities based on your values.

Just a few minutes of intentional thought every morning will allow you to focus your energy, increase your influence, and make your day all that it can be!

Each journal in the series has different motivational quotes and a motivational theme. Choose one or get all six for an entire year's worth of **Motivational Planning**!

Order books online at Amazon or RiaStory.com

Note: *Leadership Gems is the generic, non-gender specific, version of Leadership Gems for Women. The content is very similar.*

Women are naturally high impact leaders because they are relationship oriented. However, it's a *"man's world"* out there and natural ability isn't enough to help you be successful as a leader. You must be intentional.

Ria packed these books with 30 leadership gems which very successful people internalize and apply. Ria has combined her years of experience in leadership roles of different organizations along with years of studying, teaching, training, and speaking on leadership to give you these 30, short and simple, yet powerful and profound, lessons to help you become very successful, regardless of whether you are in a formal leadership position or not.

Order books online at Amazon or RiaStory.com

You have hopes, dreams, and goals you want to achieve. You have aspirations of leaving a legacy of significance. You have untapped potential waiting to be unleashed. But, unfortunately, how to maximize your potential isn't something addressed in job or skills training. And sadly, how to achieve success and find significance in life isn't something taught in school, college, or by most parents.

In *ACHIEVE: Maximize Your Potential with 7 Keys to Unlock Success and Significance*, Ria shares lessons to help you become more influential, more successful and maximize your potential in life. Three-page chapters are short, yet powerful, and provide principles on realizing your potential with actionable takeaways. These brief vignettes provide humorous, touching, or sad lessons straight from the heart that you can immediately apply to your own situation.

Order books online at Amazon or RiaStory.com

Become inspired by this 30-day collection of daily devotions for women, where you will find practical advice on intentionally living with a grateful heart, inspirational quotes, short journaling opportunities, and scripture from God's Word on practicing gratitude.

Order books online at Amazon or RiaStory.com

Ria's *Effective Leadership Series* books are written to develop and enhance your leadership skills, while also helping you increase your abilities in areas like communication and relationships, time management, planning and execution, leading and implementing change. Look for more books in the *Effective Leadership Series*:

- *Straight Talk: The Power of Effective Communication*
- *PRIME Time: The Power of Effective Planning*
- *Change Happens: Leading Yourself and Others through Change (Co-authored by Ria & Mack Story)*
- *Leadership Gems & Leadership Gems for Women*

Read books by Mack Story

High impact leaders align their habits with key values in order to maximize their influence. High impact leaders intentionally grow and develop themselves in an effort to more effectively grow and develop others. These *10 Values* are commonly understood. However, they are not always commonly practiced. These *10 Values* will help you build trust and accelerate relationship building. Those mastering these *10 Values* will be able to lead with speed as they develop 360° of influence from wherever they are.

Order books online at Amazon or TopStoryLeadership.com

Are you looking for transformation in your life? Do you want better results? Do you want stronger relationships?

In *Defining Influence*, Mack breaks down many of the principles that will allow anyone at any level to methodically and intentionally increase their positive influence.

Mack blends his personal growth journey with lessons on the principles he learned along the way. He's not telling you what he learned after years of research, but rather what he learned from years of application and transformation. Everything rises and falls on influence.

Order books online at Amazon or TopStoryLeadership.com

10 Foundational Elements of Intentional Transformation serves as a source of motivation and inspiration to help you climb your way to the next level and beyond as you learn to intentionally create a better future for yourself. The pages will ENCOURAGE, ENGAGE, and EMPOWER you as you become more focused and intentional about moving from where you are to where you want to be.

All of us are somewhere, but most of us want to be somewhere else. However, we don't always know how to get there. You will learn how to intentionally move forward as you learn to navigate the 10 foundational layers of transformation.

Order books online at Amazon or TopStoryLeadership.com

"Sales persuasion and influence, moving others, has changed more in the last 10 years than it has in the last 100 years. It has transitioned from buyer beware to seller beware" ~ Daniel Pink

So, it's no longer *"Buyer beware!"* It's *"Seller beware!"* Why? Today, the buyer has the advantage over the seller. Most often, they are holding it in their hand. It's a smart phone. They can learn everything about your product before they meet you. They can compare features and prices instantly. The major advantage you do still have is: YOU! IF they like you. IF they trust you. IF they feel you want to help them. This book is filled with 30 short chapters providing unique insights that will give you the advantage, not over the buyer, but over your competition: those who are selling what you're selling. It will help you sell yourself.

Order books online at Amazon or TopStoryLeadership.com

It's easier to compete when you're attracting great people instead of searching for good people. *Blue-Collar Leadership® & Culture* will help you understand why culture is the key to becoming a sought after employer of choice within your industry and in your area of operation.

You'll also discover how to leverage the components of The Transformation Equation to create a culture that will support, attract, and retain high performance team members.
Blue-Collar Leadership® & Culture is intended to serve as a tool, a guide, and a transformational road map for leaders who want to create a high impact culture that will become their greatest competitive advantage

Order books online at Amazon or BlueCollarLeadership.com

Are you ready to play at the next level and beyond?

In today's high stakes game of business, the players on the team are the competitive advantage for any organization. But, only if they are on the field instead of on the bench.

The competitive advantage for every individual is developing 360° of influence regardless of position, title, or rank.

Blue-Collar Leadership® & *Teamwork* provides a simple, yet powerful and unique, resource for individuals who want to increase their influence and make a high impact. It's also a resource and tool for leaders, teams, and organizations, who are ready to Engage the Front Line to Improve the Bottom Line.

Order books online at Amazon or BlueCollarLeadership.com

"I wish someone had given me these books 30 years ago when I started my career on the front lines. They would have changed my life then. They can change your life now." ~ Mack Story

Blue-Collar Leadership® & Supervision and *Blue-Collar Leadership®* are written specifically for those who lead the people on the frontlines and for those on the front lines. With 30 short, easy to read 3 page chapters, these books contain powerful, yet simple to understand leadership lessons.

Download the first 5 chapters of each book FREE at: BlueCollarLeadership.com/download

Order books online at Amazon or BlueCollarLeadership.com

Fast and Effective Workforce & Leadership Development for Team Members and Leaders at Every Level

Leaders are **BUSY**. The greatest challenge High Impact leaders face in leadership development is the struggle to find time.

Workforce development is **critical** for creating a leadership culture that attracts, retains, and engages top talent. Unfortunately however, opportunities for growth, team building, and leadership development are often pushed aside, second to project deadlines, customer needs, and urgent job details.

That's why Mack Story designed *Toolbox Tips*, a collection of powerful leadership principles delivered in a short and easy to understand format for quick and consistent workforce development.

Order books online at Amazon or BlueCollarLeadership.com

The biggest challenge in process improvement and cultural transformation isn't identifying the problems. It's execution: implementing and sustaining the solutions.

Blue-Collar Kaizen is a resource for anyone in any position who is, or will be, leading a team through process improvement and change. Learn to engage, empower, and encourage your team for long term buy-in and sustained gains.

Mack Story has over 11,000 hours experience leading hundreds of leaders and thousands of their cross-functional kaizen team members through process improvement, organizational change, and cultural transformation.

Order books online at Amazon or TopStoryLeadership.com

"I wish someone had given me these books 30 years ago when I started my career. They would have changed my life then. They can change your life now." ~ Mack Story

MAXIMIZE Your Potential will help you learn to lead yourself well. *MAXIMIZE Your Leadership Potential* will help you learn to lead others well. With 30 short, easy to read 3 page chapters, these books contain simple and easy to understand, yet powerful leadership lessons.

Note: These two MAXIMIZE books are the white-collar, or non-specific, version of the Blue-Collar Leadership® books and contain nearly identical content.

Become The Leader You Are Destined To Be℠

Ria Story
Leadership Speaker, Trainer, & Author

Increase Your Influence. Develop Your Leadership. Maximize Your Results.

Ria Story is empowering women to become the leaders they are destined to be℠ with leadership development content specifically designed for women.

Ria teaches leadership and success principles in a real, relatable, and practical way helping you increase your influence, develop your leadership, and maximize your results.

Sexually abused by her father from age 12-19 and trafficked by him, Ria left home at 19 without a job, money, or a high school diploma. Realizing the biggest obstacle to success is embracing excuses, Ria set her goals high and worked to achieve them. Today, as a TEDx speaker, author, and certified leadership trainer with nearly 20 years of experience in addition to her MBA and several other management degrees, Ria shares the lessons she learned to be successful and influence people.

Fearfully and *Wonderfully* Me
Become The Leader You Are Destined To Be

334.332.3526
Ria@RiaStory.com
LinkedIn/In/RiaStory

RiaStory.com

MAXIMIZE YOUR RESULTS IN LIFE AND LEADERSHIP

- Leadership Development
- Personal Growth
- Communication/Trust/Relationships
- Time Management/Planning/Execution
- Managing Change/Transformation
- Custom Programs Available

What clients have to say…

"My first words are, GET SIGNED UP! This training is not, and I stress, not your everyday leadership seminar! I have attended dozens and sent hundreds to the so-called 'Leadership-Training.' I can tell you that while all of the courses, classes, webinars, and seminars, had good intentions, nothing can touch what Mack and Ria Story provide. I just wish I had it 20 years ago!"
~ **Sam McLamb, VP & COO, CMP**

"I am using your material to empower myself and my female clients. Thanks for sharing your story and a wonderful journey of growth!"
~ **Sue Q, Licensed Clinical Therapist**

"It was awesome! Ria has a real gift. I came away with so many helpful tools! Thank you Ria!"
~ **Stefanie, Workshop Attendee**

Get the Tools You Need to Increase Your Influence, Develop Your Leadership, and Maximize Your Results.

Special Offer!

FOR A LIMITED TIME, Ria is offering a special speaking or training package. Take advantage of the special offer with a reduced speaking/training fee of only $5,400 and receive:

- Up to 2 hours of on-site speaking or training
- 300 copies of one or more of her books FREE!
- For details, topics, and programs visit: RiaStory.com/SpecialOffer

**Call today! Deals like this don't last forever!
334.332.3526 or visit RiaStory.com**

"My first words are, GET SIGNED UP! This training is not, and I stress, not your everyday leadership seminar...nothing can touch what Mack and Ria Story provide!"
~ Sam McLamb, VP & COO

334.332.3526
Ria@RiaStory.com

www.ingramcontent.com/pod-product-compliance
Lightning Source LLC
Chambersburg PA
CBHW051536240526
45465CB00027B/271